ANNA SUI

FASHION IDEA BOOK

Whenever I accomplish one of my dreams,
I think it's time to come up with a new dream.

I like black every season; it's always cool, always appropriate, always rock and roll.

Make an effort, opt for a little glamour, experiment
with new ideas, have fun, don't take yourself
so seriously.

I love the excitement of finding something new; that extraordinary moment of inspiration that changes you forever.

This is my gift to you from my heart: the perfect personification of everything I've always believed in . . . a fantasy of an exotic past and the hope for a romantic future.

I remember wanting to be a fashion designer even before I really knew what one was.

I find it so important to maintain a spark of curiosity, the thrill of adventure, the charm of an unexpected surprise.

These are the colors of my memories and dreams.

I keep my eyes open.

Instead of waiting for my dreams to come true one day in the future, I decided to start behaving as if I am already living in that world.

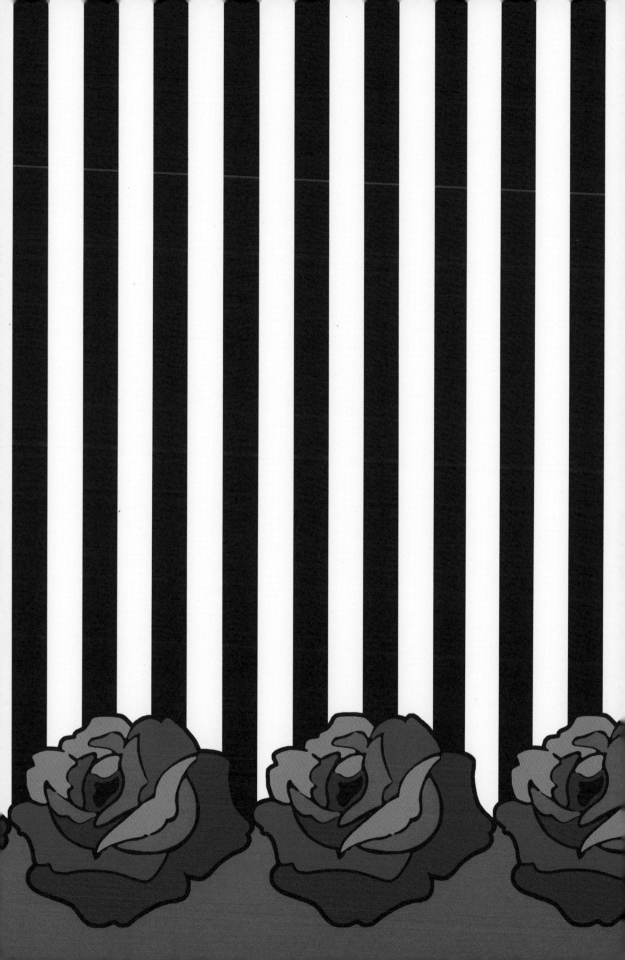

Music infuses everything I do.

I'm all about the romanticism of the past mixed with the vitality of rock and roll.

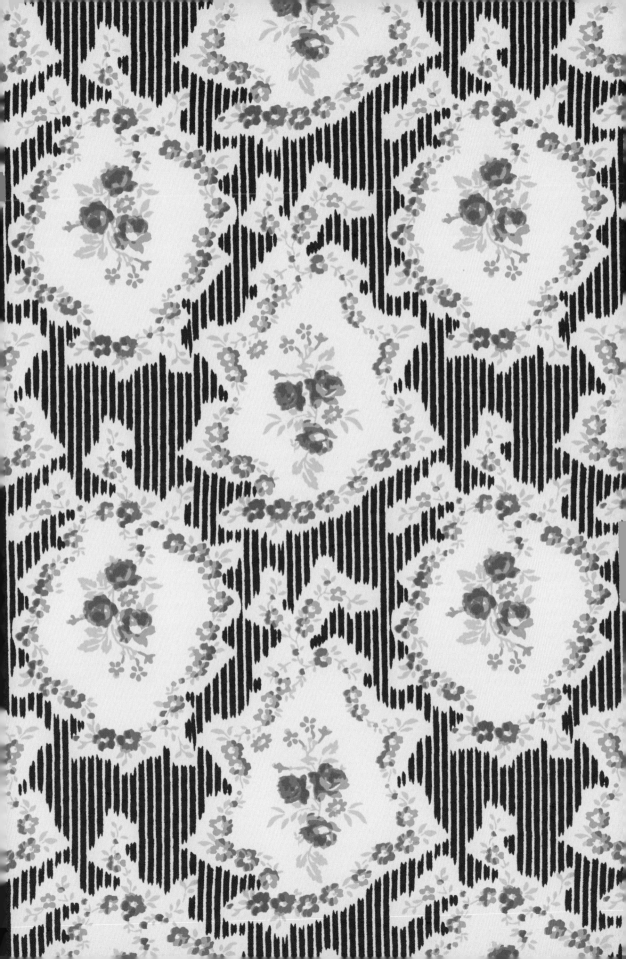

Dreams can carry a person further than anything else.

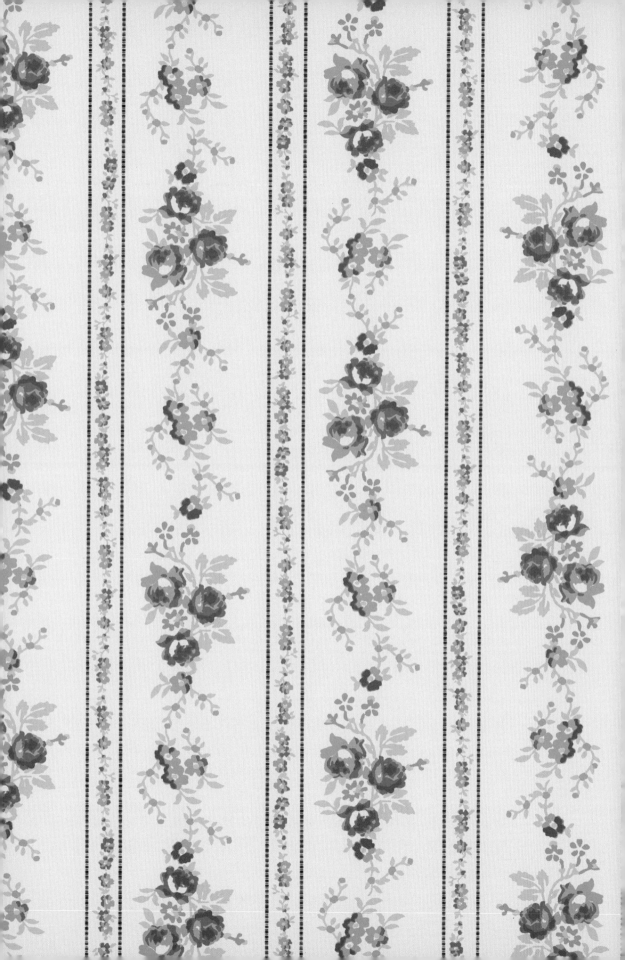

The flea market is like taking a trip on a magic carpet to exotic places and times . . . you never know what you'll discover.

I've got the best job in the world, because I'm allowed to get inspired by what I like.

Be true to yourself. Do what you are best at and learn your craft.

My motto has always been "Live Your Dream."